CONTENTS

Why should I go to bed now?	4
How does my brain work?	7
Why should I eat breakfast?	10
How can exercise help?	14
Why shouldn't I watch TV all day?	18
What is stress?	20
How can I stop stress?	22
Why should I talk about my feelings?	24
How can I feel good about myself?	27
Amazing facts about the brain	29
Glossary	30
Further reading	31
Index	32

Keep a diary

Throughout the book, there are ideas for keeping a diary. This will be a record of what you eat and the exercises that you take, and what was good for your brain. You can add your own notes to the diary, too.

Words appearing in the text in bold, **like this**, are explained in the Glossary.

WHY SHOULD I GO TO BED NOW?

Did you know that you can survive longer without food than you can without sleep? Your body needs the rest it gets while you sleep to recover from the day's activities – and sleep is vital for a healthy mind.

It is when your mind is busy at night that you dream – although you only remember a dream if you wake up while you are having one.

Why does my mind need sleep?

When we talk about your mind, we mean your thoughts, feelings, memories and moods. Your brain is the part of your body that controls your mind. Unlike most of your body, your brain does not rest while you sleep – it still has to control your heartbeat, breathing and other body functions. Scientists think that your brain uses your sleeping time to solve problems, and to sort out the various experiences and new information you learned during the day.

WHY SHOULD I GO TO BED NOW?

+ and other questions about a healthy mind +

Heinemann
LIBRARY

Louise Spilsbury

www.heinemann.co.uk/library

Visit our website to find out more information about **Heinemann Library** books.

To order:

☎ Phone 44 (0) 1865 888066

▤ Send a fax to 44 (0) 1865 314091

▣ Visit the Heinemann Bookshop at www.heinemann.co.uk/library to browse our catalogue and order online.

First published in Great Britain by Heinemann Library, Halley Court, Jordan Hill, Oxford OX2 8EJ, part of Harcourt Education. Heinemann is a registered trademark of Harcourt Education Ltd.

Editorial: Nancy Dickmann, Jennifer Tubbs and Louise Galpine
Design: David Poole and Tokay Interactive Ltd (www.tokay.co.uk)
Illustrations: Kamae Design Ltd
Picture Research: Rebecca Sodergren and Liz Eddison
Production: Séverine Ribierre and Jonathan Smith

Originated by Ambassador Litho Ltd
Printed in China by W K T

ISBN 0 431 11097 2 (hardback)
07 06 05 04 03
10 9 8 7 6 5 4 3 2 1

ISBN 0 431 11107 3 (paperback)
08 07 06 05 04
10 9 8 7 6 5 4 3 2 1

British Library Cataloguing in Publication Data

Spilsbury, Louise
Why Should I Go to Bed Now? and other questions about a healthy mind
616.8'9
A full catalogue record for this book is available from the British Library.

Acknowledgements

Corbis pp. **9** (Bob Winsett), **10** (Gerhard Steiner), **16** (Tom Stewart), **20** (Maurizio Valdarnini), **24** (Huerwitz Creative), **27** (Randy O'Rourke), **28** (RF); Getty Images pp. **14**, **15**, **21**, **23** (Imagebank) **4**, **6**, **19**, **25** (Stone) **11**, **17** (Taxi); Rex Features p.**26** (John Powell); Science Photo Library pp. **5**, **13**, **18**; Tudor Photography pp. **12**, **22**.

Cover photograph of child in bed, reproduced with permission of Tudor Photography.

The publishers would like to thank Julie Johnson for her assistance in the preparation of this book.

Every effort has been made to contact copyright holders of any material reproduced in this book. Any omissions will be rectified in subsequent printings if notice is given to the publishers.

What happens when I sleep?

When you fall asleep, your brain tells your body to gradually relax until, after about an hour, you are in a deep sleep. Your body is very still – except for your eyes! At times during your sleep, your eyes move around quickly, as if they are following the thoughts in your mind. This is called REM (rapid eye movement) sleep, and it is when we dream.

HOW MUCH SLEEP DO I NEED?

You need different amounts of sleep at different stages in your life. Babies sleep for about sixteen hours a day; teenagers need about eight hours, while older people may only need six hours. Young people need up to ten hours sleep, but you may find that you need more or less.

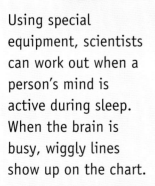

Using special equipment, scientists can work out when a person's mind is active during sleep. When the brain is busy, wiggly lines show up on the chart.

TIPS FOR A GOOD NIGHT'S SLEEP

If you have trouble getting to sleep at night, try these top tips.

- Try to go to bed at roughly the same time each day, to get your body into a routine.

- Have a warm bath to relax you before bedtime.

- Have a warm milky drink, and avoid drinking tea, coffee or cola late in the day, because these can keep you awake.

- Reading a book or listening to a tape helps some people to drop off.

Missing out on sleep can mean missing out on a lot of fun or learning the following day. Sleep is vital for keeping your body and mind healthy and happy.

What happens if you do not get enough sleep?

When you do not get enough sleep, you feel tired and grumpy, and you may act a little clumsily. You may have trouble concentrating on your schoolwork, or find that you squabble more with your friends.

HOW DOES MY BRAIN WORK?

Your brain is like a living computer, but one that is far more powerful and clever than any machine. Every moment of the day, whether you are sleeping or swotting, your brain is dealing with a huge range of complicated tasks.

The brain is the control centre of your body. It looks a bit like a big, grey, wrinkly walnut, and it is made up of different parts, each with a different job to do. **Nerves** are like your body's private telephone system. Messages travel to your brain from the rest of your body – and back again – along nerves that pass through your spinal cord (inside your backbone).

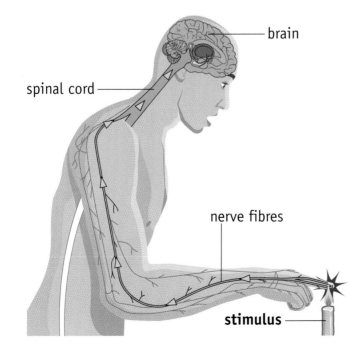

brain

spinal cord

nerve fibres

stimulus

Information about the world around you passes from your senses, along nerve fibres in your spinal cord and to your brain. Your brain stores this information so you can learn from your experiences.

The parts of a brain

The cerebrum is the largest part of the brain. It does most of your thinking, based on information from your senses, and tells the rest of your body what to do. It has two halves. The right half controls the left side of your body and the left half controls the right side.

The hypothalamus sits beneath the thalamus. It controls your body temperature, and deals with sensations such as hunger or tiredness.

The thalamus sorts out the nerve signals that come through the brain stem. It sends them to the different parts of the brain.

The cerebellum controls your automatic body movements, such as balancing your body when you ride a bike.

The hippocampus is a tiny, but important, part of the cerebrum. It deals with memories – of things that happened recently and of things that happened long ago.

The brain stem connects the rest of the brain to the spinal cord. It controls basic body functions, such as breathing, your **circulation system** and **digestion**.

How does my mind work?

The outer layer of the brain's cerebrum is called the cerebral cortex. Scientists believe that this is the part that is responsible for your thoughts and feelings. Your cerebral cortex does the work when you write a school essay, draw a picture, design a brick model or imagine your future.

To have a healthy mind, you need to take care of the body part that controls it – your brain. The bones of your skull form a protective box around your brain, but you should still wear a helmet when you ride a bike or skateboard.

MIND-BOGGLING

People use a lot of different phrases about the mind. If you have a 'clear head' or you can 'think straight', it means that your mind feels up to dealing with the task ahead. When you need to 'clear your mind', you feel muddled and need some time to focus.

WHY SHOULD I EAT BREAKFAST?

No one expects a battery-operated toy to work without batteries or a car to start without petrol. Your brain is a kind of natural machine. Like the rest of your body, it needs fuel to give it **energy** to work properly. Your body fuel is food and, after a long night without eating, your body is in urgent need of recharging!

Breakfast boost

Think of the many ways you use your brain in a morning at school – it helps you to talk, read, do maths, answer questions and write. Tests have shown that pupils who skip breakfast cannot concentrate on their morning lessons as well as those who have had a good breakfast.

A fast is when you go without food for a long time. By morning, it can be about fourteen hours since you last ate. You need to 'break your fast' to recharge your brain and body.

How does breakfast help?

When you eat, your body turns food into energy by a process called **digestion**. This is when food is broken down in your stomach and intestines. Most of the food we eat is broken down into **glucose**, a kind of sugar. The glucose passes into your blood and is carried to all parts of your body, including your brain. Your body uses glucose to make the energy it needs to work properly.

Some body parts, such as muscles, can store glucose for later, but your brain needs a constant supply. After a night without food, your brain's glucose levels are very low, and it needs a new supply to get it going again.

Your brain is the greediest part of your body. When it is working hard, it uses up more energy than even your heart, which has to pump blood all around your body 24 hours a day.

What makes a healthy breakfast?

Like any other meal, your breakfast should include a mix of the five **nutrients** to be healthy. **Carbohydrates** – found in cereals, bread, bagels, muffins, rice and grains – are very important. The body converts these into **glucose**, to give you **energy** all morning. Dairy products – such as milk, eggs, cheese, nuts and peanut butter – give you some **protein**, **minerals** and a little **fat**. A glass of fruit juice or a piece of fruit gives you your morning dose of **vitamins**.

If you are too busy to eat breakfast, make a change. Get up fifteen minutes earlier, or pack a breakfast and eat it on your way!

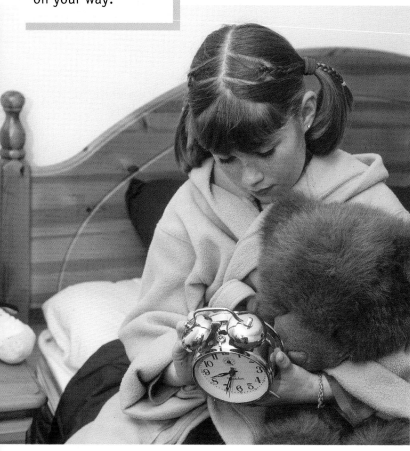

The important thing is to have a mix of nutrients – it does not matter what you eat. If cold pizza, beans on toast, a tuna sandwich or even a bowl of soup get you started, then go for it!

Keep a diary

Keep a record of what you eat for breakfast for two weeks. Then look back and work out if you were feeding your brain a good variety of nutrients, and mark each breakfast out of ten. What can you do to improve your breakfast choices in future?

This special picture of a brain shows the large area of fluid inside it (the yellow and red parts). As your brain uses this liquid, you need to help to top it up again by drinking plenty of water.

Water on the brain

Do not forget to drink lots of water, too. You might not be able to hear it sloshing about when you move your head, but your brain contains lots of liquid, called cerebrospinal fluid. Your brain needs this fluid to work properly. You need to drink at least six glasses of water a day to stay healthy.

HOW CAN EXERCISE HELP?

Have you ever heard someone say that they were going for a walk 'to clear their head'? It is a fact that your 'head' – your mind – often feels sharper and more alert after exercise. Scientists are still puzzling over exactly why this might be, but most believe that it is because exercise increases the amount of **glucose** and **oxygen** that gets to your brain, so it has more **energy**.

When you exercise you breathe faster to take in more oxygen from the air.

Why does walking clear my head?

When you walk, your leg muscles need extra energy, which they make using glucose from your food and oxygen from the air. Your body collects more oxygen from the air by breathing faster. Your heart beats faster to pump the blood, which carries the glucose and oxygen, around your **circulation system** – the blood vessels all over your body.

As the blood passes through your brain, it receives an extra dose of oxygen and glucose, too. Your brain uses these to produce energy. As blood passes through the different parts of the body, it also collects waste left over from energy production. Blood travelling through the brain removes waste, so your brain really should feel clearer after exercise!

Exercise for relaxation

Exercise also helps your brain because it helps you to relax. This might seem like a contradiction, because we have just seen how exercise makes your mind more alert. Although straight after exercising your brain feels more active, later you feel relaxed. Your body is tired out, so you sleep more soundly – and getting a good night's sleep is important for a healthy mind.

Do not exercise right before bedtime, because this can keep you awake. Allow your body a couple of hours to wind down after you have been active.

15

Think positive!

Exercise also helps you to think and feel more positive about things. This is because, when you are active, your body releases chemicals called endorphins. These produce a feeling of well-being or happiness in your brain. When you feel happier and more positive, you can get on better with people, schoolwork and the rest of your life.

Keep a diary

Keep a record in your diary of the exercise you do each day for two weeks. Note down your mood, and how clear your mind felt before and after you exercised. When you look back over the fortnight, did you find that exercise was good for your brain?

Exercise can change your mood! It can take your mind off your troubles, and it increases the amount of chemicals that create positive feelings in the brain.

16

Which exercise is best?

It does not really matter what sort of exercise you do – just choose activities that you enjoy, and try to do several different things each week. This can include walking to school or to a friend's house each day, a dance class, a swim, a cycle ride and a PE lesson. It is not hard to find ways to get enough exercise – try to do about 20 minutes every day.

> Exercise – alone or in a team – makes your mind and your body fitter.

Team sports

There are times when team sports can have a negative effect on your mind. This happens when games become too competitive and people feel unhappy if their team loses or if they let the team down. Most of the time, playing in a team makes people feel more positive. As well as exercising, it is great to share experiences with other people. It is also a good way to make new friends.

WHY SHOULDN'T I WATCH TV ALL DAY?

Like any other part of your body, your brain needs exercise to keep it healthy. Watching TV is okay sometimes, but your brain needs a mix of activities to be on top form.

Making connections

This picture shows brain neurons. The blobs are the main parts of the nerve cells, and the lines are fibres that carry electrical signals.

Your brain is made up of millions of **nerve cells**, called neurons, which look like tiny bundles of fibres. When you are born, you have all your neurons, but most are not connected (joined up) to each other. When you learn or do something new, **electrical signals** carry information between the neurons. This connects them, making pathways for more signals to pass along. This is why it may seem hard when you try something new, such as swimming, but it seems easy once you have learned to do it – because the neuron connections have all been made.

What are the best brain boosters?

Different areas of your brain are responsible for different activities. Because of this, if you only do one thing, you will only exercise one part of your brain. It is important to do lots of different activities. As well as doing activities that you might expect to exercise your brain – such as reading and drawing – just trying out new sights, sounds and smells will also stimulate it.

BRAIN BOOSTERS

Doing things differently creates new pathways between neurons, and exercises neurons that are not used much. Try these brain boosters:

- Take a new route to your friend's house.
- Brush your teeth with the hand that you do not normally use.
- Learn some card tricks, or try juggling.
- Eat some spicy foods that you have not tried before.

Try solving crosswords or other brainteasers to get your brain working.

WHAT IS STRESS?

Have you ever found it hard to get to sleep because of a test or exam? Have you ever felt upset or sick because you were so worried about an argument you had with a friend? This is what it is like to feel stress. It is not only adults who can feel stressed – young people can, too.

How does stress feel?

You feel stress when you are worried, afraid or angry about something for a long time. These thoughts and feelings build up in your mind until they make your body feel ill. Some people say that stress gives them a headache or a stomach-ache, or makes it hard to relax and go to sleep at bedtime.

When people are stressed, they often say that the problem is 'playing on their mind' – they cannot think of anything else and they find it hard to concentrate.

Can some stress be good?

In certain situations, a little stress can be useful –
for example, before you perform in a school
show. When you feel nervous, your body makes
a chemical called adrenaline. It makes your heart
beat faster and you breathe
more quickly, so that you
can make **energy** faster.
This makes you more alert
and ready for action.

The problem is that other
parts of your body slow
down, to provide you with
the extra energy you need
to deal with the stress. You
do not eat or sleep so well,
and your body becomes
weaker. This means that
you are more likely to
catch **infections** that make
you ill.

Do you feel butterflies in your tummy when you
are worried about something? It happens because
blood is rushing to your brain, where you are
using a lot of energy, and away from your
stomach, leaving it feeling strange and fluttery.

HOW CAN I STOP STRESS?

If you feel stressed because you have lots of homework and activities after school, make a timetable. You can check it each day to make sure that you do all you need to do – so you can stop worrying.

The first step in dealing with stress is deciding what is causing it. Then you can work out how to cope with it. Stress is often caused by things you can change – for example, if you are having trouble with homework or a subject at school.

If you are worried about an exam or a performance, one of the best remedies is practice. If you are well-prepared, you will feel better. If you are stuck on schoolwork, ask for help. If you keep forgetting to do your homework, write a note or make a timetable, to remind you to get the work done when you need to.

What else can help?

Some of the things you should be doing to keep your whole body well – eating healthy food, getting enough sleep and taking exercise – will also help you to keep on top of stress. Many people find that taking up a new hobby can also help. It could be something restful, such as knitting or sketching, or giving yourself a new challenge, such as learning a new instrument or joining a band.

Do not overdo it though. Having too much to get through in a week can become a cause of stress, rather than help you to beat it. Make sure that you have some time to relax as well, perhaps by reading a book or just soaking in the bath.

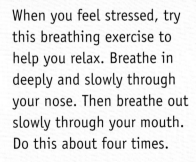

When you feel stressed, try this breathing exercise to help you relax. Breathe in deeply and slowly through your nose. Then breathe out slowly through your mouth. Do this about four times.

WHY SHOULD I TALK ABOUT MY FEELINGS?

As you near **puberty** – the teenage years when you change from a child to an adult – it is perfectly natural to have more mood changes. Sometimes you may feel angry or upset without really knowing why. If you discuss a problem with someone, it often makes you feel better.

Some people find that writing or drawing about their feelings is a helpful way of working through them.

How does talking help?

When you talk to someone about a problem, they may be able to help you to solve it. Talking about your feelings also makes you feel better because it releases some of the stress that can make you feel ill. Sometimes, you need to find other ways of dealing with your feelings. If you can feel yourself losing your temper, try counting to ten or walking away from the situation.

Who should I talk to?

It can help to talk to friends – you may find it a comfort to know that they feel just like you do sometimes. When something is really bothering you, though, it is better to talk to a parent or to another adult who cares for you, because they have more experience. They also care about you very much – even if they get cross with you sometimes.

Pick a time to talk with someone when they are not busy, and make sure that you do not get interrupted.

If you do not want to talk to someone in your family, talk to a teacher or to someone else you trust, such as a school nurse. If you prefer, you could call a free helpline, which you can find in most telephone directories. These are open day and night, and the people who answer them give advice about any problem.

25

What can I do about bullying?

Many children are made to feel unhappy or stressed because of bullying at some point in their school lives. Bullies are people who hurt others by calling them names, or by hitting them or pushing them around.

It can be difficult to know what to do about bullying. Some people find that, if they ignore the bully, he or she gets bored and leaves them alone. This is not always the case. You may need to talk to an adult you can trust, such as a parent or a teacher. They should be able to organize someone to talk to the bully, to stop them behaving in this way. This is not telling tales – bullying is wrong, and it is right and important that it is stopped.

If you see someone being teased or bullied, talk to a teacher about it when no one else is around.

HOW CAN I FEEL GOOD ABOUT MYSELF?

Feeling good about yourself and proud of who you are is called self-esteem. Self-esteem is very important to keep you both happy and healthy.

How do I get self-esteem?

Self-esteem is not something you are born with or something you can buy. People learn a lot of self-esteem from parents, carers or teachers. You can also improve your own self-esteem.

- Pat yourself on the back when you do something right, and do not dwell on things you do wrong. If you fail a test, think about what you are good at.

- Be realistic. Nobody is perfect, and we need to accept the things we cannot change.

- Play for fun, not just to win.

- Take up a new hobby – you may be really good at it.

Self-esteem gives you the courage to make new friends and to try new challenges.

What if I make mistakes?

If you do something wrong, that does not mean that you are a bad person. We live in a world where adverts and films show perfect people living perfect lives – and when real life turns out to be different, it would be easy to think that something is wrong. In real life, everyone makes mistakes, and mistakes are an important part of how we develop. You should never feel a failure because of mistakes you make. Just make sure that you learn from them.

When you have good self-esteem, you are less likely to make serious mistakes. When you respect and trust your own judgement, you will have the confidence to say no, if someone suggests doing something that you know is wrong.

AMAZING FACTS ABOUT THE BRAIN

- When you are born, your brain is about one-quarter of its adult size.

- You have about 100 billion **nerve cells** in your brain. That is about as many stars as there are in a galaxy!

- Messages travelling from your body parts to your brain through your spinal cord (backbone) travel at more than 300 kilometres per hour – as fast as the fastest trains.

- The world's heaviest-known brain weighed 2.3 kilograms. It belonged to a man who was 30 years old.

- The skull that protects your brain sounds like a single bone but, in fact, it is made up of 28 different bones that all fit together perfectly.

- Although your brain can tell you about things that your skin feels, it cannot feel things itself. Doctors can operate on a brain while the patient is awake, and the patient does not feel any pain.

GLOSSARY

carbohydrates   kind of food that gives you energy

circulation system   blood vessels (tubes) around your body, through which your blood circulates

digestion   way the body breaks down food

electrical signals   way that information passes invisibly through nerves or wires

energy   energy allows living things to do everything they need to live and grow

fat   nutrient found in foods, such as butter and oil

glucose   sugar that our bodies use to make energy

infection   kind of disease that can be caught by other people

mineral   chemical found in rocks and soil

muscles   parts of your body that pull on the bones to make them move

nerve cells   building blocks of nerves in the body

nerves   these carry messages to and from the brain

nutrients   chemicals in food that are good for you

oxygen   gas in the air that we need to breathe

proteins   substances in some of the foods we eat that our bodies can use to build or repair body parts

puberty   stage in life when your body rapidly develops to become an adult instead of a child

stimulus   something that triggers a response, often from your senses

vitamin   nutrient found in certain foods that your body needs to be healthy

FURTHER READING

Brain Surgery For Beginners And Other Major Operations For Minors, Steve Parker and David West (Simon and Schuster Young Books, 1993)

The Young Oxford Book Of The Human Being: The Body, The Mind and the Way We Live, David Glover (Oxford University Press, 1996)

Why Do I Get Toothache? And Other Questions About Nerves, Angela Royston (Heinemann, 2002)

INDEX

adrenaline 21

brain 4, 7-9, 10, 11, 13, 14, 15, 16, 18-19, 21, 29
brain boosters 19
brain parts 8
breakfast 10-11, 12
breathing exercise 23
bullying 26
butterflies in your tummy 21

cerebral cortex 9

dreams 4

endorphins 16
energy 10, 11, 12, 14, 15, 21
exams 20, 22
exercise 14-17, 18, 19, 23

food 10-13, 23

glucose 11, 12, 14, 15

heart 11, 14
helplines 25
hobbies 23, 27

infections and illness 21, 24

mind 4, 9, 14, 17, 20, 28
mistakes, making 28
mood changes 24
muscles 11, 14

nerves 7
neurons (nerve cells) 18, 19, 29
nutrients 12

oxygen 14, 15

positive thinking 16
puberty 24

relaxation 6, 15, 23

schoolwork 6, 16, 22
self-esteem 27, 28
sleep 4-6, 15, 23
stress 20-3, 24, 26

talking about feelings 24-5
team sports 17
temper, controlling 24

water 13